FLYING THE ZUNI MOUNTAINS

by Ann Darr

Forest Woods Media Productions Inc.
The Bunny and the Crocodile Press

Washington, D.C.

Library of Congress Card Number: 94-071525
International Standard Book Number: 0-938572-08-3

First edition printed 1994
Second edition printed 1996
Printed in the U.S.A.

Typography by Cynthia Comitz, *In Support* Graphics

Printing by George Klear, *Printing Press Inc.*

This book is made possible in part by the D.C. Commission
on the Arts & Humanities and the National Endowment for
the Arts. We are grateful for the support of these agencies.

For information, contact:
Forest Woods Media Productions Inc.
c/o 4902 Falstone Avenue
Chevy Chase, MD 20815

This book is dedicated to all Women Pilots
particularly to the WASP
members of 44-W-3
on this, the 50th anniversary year
of our graduation, receiving of
our wings

Poems in this volume have been selected from Ann Darr's poetry collections as follows: *St Ann's Gut* (Wm Morrow 1971), *The Myth of a Woman's Fist* (Wm Morrow 1973), *Cleared For Landing* (Dryad Press 1978), *Riding With the Fireworks* (Alice James Books 1981), *Do You Take This Woman. . .* (Washington Writers Publishing House 1986), *The Twelve Pound Cigarette* (SCOP Publications 1991), *Confessions of a Skewed Romantic* (Bunny and Crocodile Press 1993).

An Old Film At The Reunion of the Fifinellas is reprinted from *Passager* 1994.

Poems appearing for the first time: Decisions, First Assignment B-26 School, Assigned to Dodge City Air Base, Stockton 1944, Transformed, Between Battles in That Sometime War, The Soldier's Body Arrives From Overseas, The Hearing 11/2/77, Chattanooga Choo Choo in Kalamazoo, Hello Spring.

The characters in the monologues in A PLAY IN FIVE FICTIVE VOICES are fiction, based on action and reaction that might have been, placed in a setting that was real, during and after WWII.

Special thanks to Kristin Swan Lent, Margaret DeBolt Christian and Cecily Elmes Kayes for sharing their photo collections. Grateful acknowledgement is made to friends and unknown photographers whose names could not be included.

CONTENTS

HONORING THE LEADERS

Now we can celebrate! Jacqueline Cochran has her United States Postage Stamp! On March 9th 1996 at the former site of Cochran's ranch, now Indian Palms Country Club and Resort, the postmaster of Indio, California presented the First Day covers before an admiring crowd of WASPs and friends. Jets and vintage planes flew overhead.

Jacqueline Cochran was the Director of the Women's Airforce Service Pilots of WWII. General Henry H. "Hap" Arnold gave her the position. She had returned from England where she had worked with the American Wing of the Air Transport Auxiliary, in the middle of summer 1942. In her flying career, she had won more flying awards than any other United States pilot, male or female.

DECISIONS

Jacqueline Cochran
used to say:
If your hands turn wet
when you face the plane
get
out of the flying game.

If there is justice in the world, there will also be a stamp for Nancy Harkness Love who headed the Women's Auxiliary Ferrying Squadron.

TELLING THE WASP STORY

Four women sat at lunch on the Upper West Side of New York City, a mother, her grown daughter and two of the daughter's professional friends. They were talking of last night's wind storm.

"I remember once in Sweetwater, Texas," said the older woman, "when the wind splattered our newly painted barracks with sand until it looked as if they had the measles."

"Sweetwater? Barracks?" said one of the young women.

"During World War II. That's where the women pilots were trained," said the older woman.

"What do you mean, women pilots in World War II," said Leslie.

"I never heard of such a thing," said Susan.

"Never heard of us? Never heard of the WASP?"

"Oh yes, WASPs. White Anglo Saxon Protestants."

"Oh no!" laughed the older woman. "We were Women Airforce Service Pilots long before the rich whites were singled out. You should have seen the angry letter I wrote to a radio commentator the first time I heard WASP used as a privileged class. I was so mad I nearly ran my VW on a curb."

"You were one of the women?" asked Leslie.

"Yes, and this is the 50th anniversary year of my class graduation."

The two younger women turned to the woman's daughter and said, almost in unison, "Why didn't you tell us?"

Deborah replied, "I wanted her to tell you herself. I've been trying to persuade her to write it all down."

"I have," said the mother. "Flight is my metaphor. It's scattered all through my poems. Flight in all of its meanings, the power dream, rising from the ashes, running away from. . ."

"But what about the women fliers?" said Leslie.

"Why was it kept a secret?" asked Susan.

"It wasn't," said the mother. "There are many books about the WASP, detailed history, the documents on file in Washington, interviews of many pilots, stories of Life after the Army."

Suddenly the woman realized what her daughter had been trying to tell her all along. In spite of all of the books, the story still needed to be told. If these two young professional women, feminists, hadn't yet heard, the story needed to be told. Every young woman making her way in the world needed to know what happened to careers of women before her.

"You were pioneers," said Susan.

"Yes," the woman said firmly. "We were pioneers. If we had not flown as we did, there would not be women flying in the Airforce today. Even though we had our wings clipped, we were the proving ground that women could fly as well as men. In some instances, even better." The woman turned to her daughter, "You set this up didn't you?"

Her daughter grinned. "You kept saying your story was not unique enough, you were just one of the group. I wanted you to hear what my generation might ask you, since you wouldn't listen to me."

"You win," her mother laughed. "I didn't really know how many times the story had to be told before it would be heard."

AUTHOR'S NOTES

This is a witness book by one of the crew, how the flying affected her life. The hope is it will bring up personal memories of the WASPs of similar experience, give pleasure in the recall. The poems (except for several) are published in previous poetry books of the author. Many books have been published about the WASP experience, history, memoirs, accomplishments, the battle inside the organization, the battle against those who did not want women in the service. This is not one of them.

When the U.S. became involved in World War II, the shortage of planes and pilots was acute. General Henry H. (Hap) Arnold spearheaded the effort to use existing licensed women pilots with at least 500 hours to do routine transport flying. In September 1942, the Women's Auxiliary Ferry Squadron (WAFS) and the Women's Flying Training Detachment (WFTD) were created, the latter to train women pilots who had fewer hours. Nancy Love was Director of the WAFS and Jacqueline Cochran Director of the WFTD. In August 1943, the two groups were merged under the designation WASP.

Twenty-five thousand women applied for the training, 1830 were accepted after rigorous testing, and 1074 won their wings. They flew more than 60 million miles in every type of plane the Army Airforce owned, in every flying task in the United States, ferrying, towing targets in gunnery schools for ground and aerial gunners, instructing, mapping unmapped territory, etc.

Because the militarization bill HB4269 did not pass Congress, the WASP were disbanded in December of 1944. Thirty-eight died in the service of their country.

Many of the WASPs' beginning flight training was with the CPT (Civilian Pilot Training). I trained at the University of Iowa where classes were made up of 10 trainees, one of which could be female. Ground school was in the Engineering Department. I was working my way through the University as a Student Girl (a helper in a home for room and board). Flying lessons were in Taylorcrafts at 6 AM, before my 8 o'clock classes. We didn't know then that the program was designed to train, as quickly as possible, pilots to supplement the small supply in case we went to war.

11

I had a childhood myth that I could fly to heaven and see my mother who had been killed in an automobile accident when I was three. The myth stuck to me as I grew, and I knew that someday I would fly. I was a prairie child. In Iowa we didn't have the oceans or the mountains, what we had was sky. It played an enormous role in my life, my imagination filled it with impossible dreaming.

Before the WASP, I was writing and performing in a radio program for NBC's Blue Network (now ABC) in New York City, *The Woman of Tomorrow* program, a half hour daily participating radio show with an interview in the middle. We focused on everything of interest to women from fashion to theatre to food to books. We were busy trying to tell them how to save sugar, tin foil, gasoline, anything to help the war effort.

There were 17 classes of women pilots, beginning in Houston as WAFS and finishing at Avenger Field, Sweetwater as WASPs. Women came from every walk of life, teachers, nurses, engineers, debutantes, mothers, wives.

This is the 50th Anniversary of the graduation of my class of 44-W-3, indicating the third class of 1944 (April 15 to be exact). Our class served as guinea pigs in that we skipped basic training and went from primary planes to advanced trainers—from PT-19s to AT-6s. If women could do it, so could the men, male pilots who were taken into the Aircorp or Airforce without previous flying training. Our class went back to the B-13 (Basic trainer) for instrument flying, and later, Instructor's Instrument Flight.

I have had the deep pleasure of re-living the flying in the writing. The exhilaration, the excitement of rising into the air, the satisfaction of making every move count, the precision of it, being in control, and the sheer joy of seeing the sweep of the earth. Flight is my metaphor, in all of its meanings. I still write flying poems although I do not fly in the pilot seat except in dreams.

I loved the camaraderie. Friends for my forever. To suffer through the anxieties of flight checks, of aching bones, of effort to do it right! Living close-in with all of its ups and downs.

The worst experience was to be thrown out with short warning. To be disregarded as if we had not made a real contribution to the war effort. To be told to be silent on our own behalf when the bill came up in the Congress that would have made us veterans. It took thirty-three years for us to be so recognized. To have to be quiet about our feelings of being badly treated (we were supposed to be "ladies"), not complain when we were victims of sexism. To have to take up a collection to send home the body of a WASP co-pilot who died in a crash because the Army said it was not responsible and Civil Service said it was not responsible.

We were Pioneers of the Women Pilots. I was one of the lucky women who were part of the experiment that proved women could fly as well as men. The Airforce was wrong in 1977 when it put out a news release saying women had just begun to fly military aircraft. The WAFS and the WASPs were flying everything the Army Airforce owned in 1942, '43, and '44. In 1977 we were finally recognized for our efforts. Although it was too late for us to be granted insurance, education and most other benefits, we were proud to be named Veterans.

BEGINNINGS

FIRST SOLO FLIGHT – CIVILIAN PILOT TRAINING – IOWA CITY 1940

We had been doing landings. Taylorcrafts had dual controls. I was working on trying to meet the ground at just the moment the plane stopped flying, the instant all lift was gone and the wheels purred along the runway. I kept dropping it too late so we bounced and bounced again in a tricky little dance. I had just landed once again off-timing, and shaking my head with frustration. He said, pull over. I looked at him to see what his mood was, whether I was going to get a verbal scrounging. He just said it again. Pull over, gesturing with his head. He began unbuckling his parachute, opened the door and stepped out. Okay, he said, it's all yours.

It was all mine all right. All my adrenaline I didn't know I had, raced through my body. Thrill. Fright. I closed my mouth that had fallen open in surprise, swallowed hard. Now? I wasn't ready yet. I barely had enough hours to legally solo. Maybe I didn't have enough. I assumed I would take a plane up by myself after I had perfected the maneuvers. The maneuvers being take-off and landing. I saw early that taking off was a piece of pie, especially on flat Iowa windless country at 6 AM. Landing was a little more complicated. A lot more complicated if you had never done it alone. I had been doing rotten landings for several days, but always with a back-up. Mr. C could take over at any moment to ward off nose-dives, one-wing-low bounces that could swivel us into a ground loop.

I heard the door click. Saw his grin. Tried to grin back. Pushed the throttle forward and roared down the runway. Pulled back on the stick and began to climb at the same time the notes climbed my throat and soared with the sound of the engine. I don't know what I sang. Probably "OH how I love to go up in a swing. . ." Maybe it was "Over the river and through the woods. . ." I'm quite sure it wasn't "Wild Blue Yonder." All I really remember is that I was FLYING! For a wild moment I wanted to keep straight up and on and watch the ground diminish below me. But I had to turn into the flight pattern, make square corners with just the right pressure on the stick to make the turn and bring the stick back to neutral, the plane would respond to delayed action. Pull back on the throttle. Keep the wings level with the rudder. Back. Back. The feelings were in my hands and arms, my back, my feet and I knew how to do it.

A PAGE FROM MY DIARY JUST AS WRITTEN
– DECEMBER 7, 1941

237 East 26th St.
New York, New York

It came today at 2:22 PM Eastern Standard Time:
The Second World War. For us.

Vincent Sheehan is talking now. Telling of Wake Island
being white sand, blue sea and friendly young Americans
working in an awful hurry.

Now it has been taken by the Japanese.

It isn't easy, he says, and it won't be over in a few
weeks and those of us who think so are as mad as the
Japanese.

We were listening to the New York Philharmonic. The news
flash.

All day the news announcers have stumbled over words in
their hurry to get the news bulletins out to the people, us.

Japanese Ambassador in Washington taking Japan's answer to
Cordell Hull.

Bringing forth a few pithy phrases from that gentleman: "Never
in my 50 years of service have I seen such infamous state-
ments from any government.

Nor did I think they could be issued by any government on
this planet."

Even as Japan was asking for more time, their troops were
preparing and their submarines were moving out for this
attack.

That's the irony of it all. More Munich.

The Japanese Ambassador in Washington burned documents in
the yard of the Embassy, shooing away American newspaper-
men who wandered in through the gate.

A Japanese council in San Francisco tried burning papers in
an ornamental fireplace.

An official car with an Argentine license pulled away from
that apartment. Maybe it means nothing at all. Maybe it does.

G sits with a map of the Pacific on his knees. It looks
awfully small.

Clare Booth said "As Gertrude Stein would say:
the world is around, is a round, is around, and is
not flat anywhere."

This war started 10 years ago when Japan moved into
Manchukuo, and has moved around the world and back
to the Pacific.

Senator Wheeler, our leading isolationist, has been
quoted as saying "We'll have to lick the hell out of
them. War's started. There's nothing else to do."

From Washington comes news Roosevelt will speak to
Congress at noon tomorrow.

We have been married one month today.

LEARNING OF THE EXISTENCE OF THE WASP
– NEW YORK CITY 1943

"You'll need your white shortie gloves today," the secretary said as I walked into the *Woman of Tomorrow* office at Radio City. That's how I learned I was to cover the Henri Bendel Shoe Show that afternoon, one of the most elegant fashion shows in the city. I supposed our gal Helen was otherwise engaged, since she was born into high fashion and I rarely wore a hat, let alone shortie whites.

That is why I was very surprised to see her as I stepped into Bendel's deep carpeting.

"Am I glad to see you!" she said, "There must have been a scheduling error, but I'm glad it happened. I need somebody to talk to!"

I wondered what she needed to talk to me about, she always seemed to be abreast of everything happening. Today she looked even more energetic, excited than usual.

"What's up?"

"Me," she said, "I'm taking flying lessons. I hocked my grandmother's jewelry to get the money, so my folks won't know, and I'm learning to fly!"

I began to laugh. "No, no," she protested. "It's true. I've found out there is a need for pilots. That Hap Arnold, you know, the General, wants women pilots for the Airforce, and he has told Jacqueline Cochran to put together a group of women pilots."

My insides flipped over. The date was March 1943. December '41 was Pearl Harbor. Everyone I knew wanted to help. But Helen? Sophisticated elegant Helen? Flying for the Airforce? But she could do anything she set her mind to. She was intelligent, energetic, accomplished, and rich. I thought she was working at the *Woman of Tomorrow* daily radio show for a lark.

"I've never heard of women in the Airforce," I said. "Tell me about it."

"Apparently it has been in the wind for some time. I don't know why it has been kept rather secret. There are women in England who are flying for the English, American women. Cochran went to study how the women there were doing it. Now General Arnold wants her to head a group in the States. So I am taking flying lessons three times a week and soon I'll have enough time to get my private flying license."

"I already have my private license," I said.

It was her turn to stare. "What?"

"I got it while I was in college. Is that all it takes?"

"Yes, now that they've lowered the time to 45 hours. It was much higher, but it was hard to find women who could get that much time in, I guess. Anyway they lowered the requirement. They'll do further training in Army planes."

"You mean I could join up?"

"Why not? Look, I have the name of the woman who is doing the recruiting right here. Why don't you talk to her."

"What is the catch? There must be a catch." But the idea of flying for the Army was becoming a possibility in my mind. My husband would be in the Navy as soon as his medical residency was completed. Why couldn't I do something more than tell our women audience how to save sugar and tinfoil. Maybe I could have a part in saving lives if the reports about that Madman in Germany were true. Rumors were becoming more frequent, about unbelievable destruction of people, devastation of whole families, of towns... My mind swung back and forth.

"If I can do it, you can do it," Helen was holding my arms. Between us there grew an excitement that kept erupting in laughter, in quick talk. The possibilities were there. Quite by accident she had heard of the project. Quite by accident, we were sent to cover the same fashion show. Or was it an accident? Otherwise we might have gone on greeting each other briefly in the office, never learning anything about the other. Now we had a mission. Everything lay ahead of us. My mind swung back to Bucks County where the goldenrod was blooming when Paris fell. Here was my chance to do something about the city of my dreams. There was a plan after all, and I was part of it.

* * * * *

It is Fall. I am packing my bags to leave New York for a place called Sweetwater, Texas. My husband, in Navy uniform now helping to outfit his ship in the Brooklyn Navy Yard, answers the phone in our apartment. It is for me. Helen. She is back in New York. She has washed out. I am numb. "Don't worry about me," she says. "I've got a job teaching primary trainers. I just couldn't handle the big stuff." I feel bad for her and I feel bad for me. If she couldn't pass the tests, how can I? But I couldn't quit before I started. I had no choice but to leave in the morning.

1944 – FIRST LONG SOLO CROSS COUNTRY
– TEXAS TO CALIFORNIA

She is headed west from Albuquerque toward Blythe Field. She will cross a small range of mountains with an Indian name – what was it? Ah, Zuni. There is a town called Zuni, but first she must cross the Zuni range and as it comes into sight, her heart nearly stops. Color. Color dances before her eyes, like rocks of rainbow, color deep, rapturous.

If I ever have to crash, let it be here.

Half a century later, she calls it back, the first sighting of the Zuni's, as she has done, over and over when she needed them.

When the women pilots of World War II were finally granted recognition and a burial place (after 33 years of trying) she had written, I have just decided not to be buried anywhere.

Now, after all, perhaps it is the place for a final landing.
Ashes to ashes.

FLYING THE ZUNI MOUNTAINS

Hold death by the heels
and tickle his nose with a feather,
for the wind is our blood
it will blow itself away.
Never a dark red rivulet trickling through the grass
beside the bolts and the pressed-wood props made in
Camden, New Jersey.

Let the engine drone a funeral dirge,
the sharp staccato when one cylinder plays alone.
The quiet , , , just the wind.
No sound when the ribs crumple,
like the old tree falling in the forest
with no one to hear,
for we are not there.
We stand and lean on a cloud
and call for another beer.

This we know:
we are the wind.
We will come back gently over the lake,
we will lash the waves and bend the trees;
we will lie side by side on the high mountains
drinking martinis and telling the old jokes over.
Never our wings will melt or crumple with heat or hardness.
This we know.
For the man who draws the blueprints, shapes the wings,
    threads the bolts, pulls the props
is not our faith.
Ours is the wind and the wind is us
and no one shall bury us ever.

We have known space not surrounded by closets and
cabbages cooking,
we have whirled rainbows over our heads;
we have owned the earth by rising from it,
never again shall we walk with ordinary feet.

The wings were shaped from a woman's weeping. . .
no other tears shall fall.

INSTRUCTIONS FOR SURVIVAL

INSTRUCTIONS FOR SURVIVAL

You women pilots are on your way
to becoming precision flyers. It's
your responsibility to remain alive. So,
it's entirely up to you.
    the decision that bailing out is necessary
    the act of leaving your plane
    the procedure during descent
    the landing.

It's never too late to jump?
Is that what you think? If it is,
you can get the idea right out of
your helmet. THE LOWEST ALTITUDE
FROM WHICH IT IS SAFE TO JUMP FROM
A PLANE IS THE LOWEST ALTITUDE
AT WHICH YOUR CHUTE WILL OPEN
EARLY ENOUGH TO PERMIT
A SAFE LANDING.

You must be free and clear
of the plane when your chute
opens and the HEADLONG DIVE IS
THE BEST METHOD OF INSURING THAT!
Your headphone should be
disconnected, and your oxygen
tube should be detached. Invert
the plane and DIVE OUT!
WHATEVER YOU DO, DO IT FAST,
BUT DO IT CALMLY. USE YOUR HEAD,
OBEY A FEW SIMPLE RULES, AND
YOU'LL HAVE NO TROUBLE.

THE MYTH OF A WOMAN'S FIST

The myth about
a woman's fist,
(putting the thumb
inside), still
makes me flex
my hand to check,
though I have known
since it was first
told to me
as solemn truth
it was a lie.

Told to me
by the man who
sent me solo
in a plane.
I had to believe
everything he
told me.
I believed
some myth about
if any part
were lie,
it all was.
So man couldn't
fly, nor woman either,
nor any bird-form
outside of birds themselves
could rise and soar
and glide.

What I learned
on that first flight
alone
was that I sing
when I'm afraid.

Perhaps it is myth
that music tries to match
the music of the spheres,
or that the impetus is praise.
Maybe all the music of the world
is to ward off fear.

HIGH DARK

The camera that takes the pictures after the fact
can focus on any black night
over Sweetwater and find me still
circling, still wheeling for the final turn,
traveling at a breakneck speed,
hunting the level invisible earth,
still unable
to land.

On that first night solo flying
swallowed by the night,
trying to cough myself up, I must trust
all night flyers to steer clear of me. . .
bats be my friends, do your counting
out of my rectangle, owls, lay over on
some branch and hoot from there,
I cannot feather my wings, I
cannot find the field.

    I must not keep on at high speed
into the black air, am I going up or down,
are the stars above me or is it my city,
Sweetwater, sweet water, bring me down.
I cannot keep speeding through air.
I dare not keep speeding through air,
there is only one place I can arrive.
On earth. No place else will accept me
with active eyes and ears.
I have become two beings, one skin
standing a space away from the other
like a picture frame. Hurtling through air
I must make decisions that stand still
so I can perform them. Or die.
    Die? Not yet. Wipe out the pictures
of my life flashing before my eyes. That is cliché
and doesn't really happen. I am obverse enough to

have it begin. Reel one. Roll one: I am being
dangled upside down on the roof of the house
I know I was born in. . . over a balcony
with a railing of tooled poles. . . looking like
New Orleans, but it stood at the end of
the only street in town and standing on
that balcony you could watch the crops go by
year after year – cornfields end on end to an horizon
that ended because the earth curved.
    My horizon is where the earth
is curving, joined in black velvet
with the space that is curving, my plane
track is curving and I must not curve, I must
set this plane down on a straight runway, on
a level plain, before the gas gives out.

Four times now I have maneuvered into place
made the proper angle to bring me nose-straight
into the flight pattern. . . four times the rows of
yellow pearls have grown in size too soon,
and I have pulled up hard and flown on, shaken
by all my errors. I have never wanted
jewels much. I have never wanted jewels so much
in all my life. o lights. o stars.
o bats. winged creatures of the night. . .
o fraud. I have no right to join you.
I donate my wings to you – I would strip
them off if I could and give you my wings
for a house. Here I give you my engine,
my lights, my instruments, my radio, my
helmet, here – have my parachute.
I have no chance to use it.
If I opened the hatch now and stepped out,
I would discover only after I started falling
which way was down. Throw everything

overboard. Deep-six it all. Government
issue be damned. But turn another corner,
bring the yellow pearls in sight. My god
don't lose the field. Let gravity work.
Keep my fellow flyers away from me. Stop
magnetism. Sweat the parachute wet
if you have to, but don't lose the field.

One last attempt. Last?
I will keep on trying until
we are flying only by riding the wind–
except this is no glider and will plummet–
stop. I have stopped the newsreel. I
have stopped time. I am diving at great speed
into the black earth, pull up, pull, make the angle
right, let down the landing gear, now now! without
the wheels I will nose over – whack the landing gear
release – in place, we are moving
for our lives, this plane and me, flaps down, level,
not on one wheel – vertigo abhors a vacuum – level – there!
there is the touch, there is that moment in time when I am
      touching
the earth again, the wheels are part of my belly, I am hugging
      the earth
I am down.

But cover both your ears, and the sound you hear
is my plane still flying lost, still circling the dark,
and I frantic, knowing only if I do not panic can I reach home,
knowing I will always be circling, lost in the dark, traveling
at high speed, know it for what it is.

FIRST ASSIGNMENT: B-26 SCHOOL
 – DODGE CITY, KANSAS

I had been practicing saluting.

WASP Darr reporting, sir.
The Commandant came from around his desk
to shake my hand.
Are you married? Yessir.
Then I don't need to give you
my single's lecture. He motioned me
to a chair. Where do you hail from?
New York City, I said.
I know only one person in New York City,
he said, her name is Alice Maslin.
I didn't blink.
She was my boss, I said.

Two hours later we were on
the golf course and I was
telling him how Alice Maslin
was the Woman of Tomorrow on the radio show,
how I wrote copy for her, how she was
re-named Nancy Booth Craig to fit
the initials for NBC.

I am practicing my golf swing.

ASSIGNED TO DODGE CITY AIR BASE

The sign over the gate said "Boot Hill Cemetery – Those
buried here were laid to rest without coffin or prayer."

She looked over the low fence to read the head markers.
Cold sweat broke from under her bangs.

In front of the headmarker was the head, and at the foot
were the feet in boots of each body laid in the ground.

She could see they were plaster, the cheeks too pink
beneath the closed eyes, but first glance was a shock.

She tried to laugh but no sound came out. The markers
read "Two Gun Pete and His Horse." "Outlaw Jake. Ran

for Sheriff 1856. Ran from Sheriff 1860." For a moment
the eyes of Outlaw Jake blinked open and shut – blue neon eyes.

One head was different. Longer hair. Smaller mouth.
Headboard read "Toothless Nell. Shot in Dancehall Brawl 1867."

And underneath: "Circumstances brought me to this end
but I had a good mother." Did she say any such thing?

Ad Astra Per Astrum. They told me it was the Kansas motto:
To the Stars Through Difficulties. And the time line

ran through Dodge City so that in Beesum Museum of music
boxes, one phonograph was playing at four o'clock, another at five.

I dreamed that night, stretched under an army blanket that
my head stared out from the top of the bed and my boots at the bottom.

I REMEMBER

I was flying alone over desert
when a Grimm-like forest
rose from the naked sand.
Mirages don't take place at thirteen thousand feet.
We were at war, but no enemy could
grow such a forest to block the way,
yet there they stood. Redwoods
were toadstool size, compared.
    I thought my eyes were liars
until I saw those trees for what they were,
forest of storms. Streaks of pelting rain
formed trunks, convoluted clouds made leaves
for enormous trees that cast a shade upon
the desert floor to terrify the shadowed on.
    I wound my way between the monster growths,
laughing aloud to let the terror out.
Dizzy with relief, vertigo I could not afford,
for to be caught, if one moved toward
me, was to risk the world.

        (Purpose of flight: to return to Texas factory
        from California field, twin-engined trainers
        for wing re-enforcement. . . Army technical
        order number five thousand seven hundred
        sixty-three, issued after required number
        of accidents caused by
        wind-torn wings.)

    I remember my loud chant:
        You don't need me!
  The requirement has been met!
        You don't need me!
        You don't need me!

STOCKTON 1944

"Silver dollars stacked in my hand
Like a full moon over my shoulder,
There'll be shoes of leather for baby's feet
Before I'm an hour older. . ."

This is war. Majors wearing white aprons behind
the bar. Two scotch and sodas from number 11. Your
whiskey's your own and your money was. They both disappear
together. But the music is sweet and all the musicians
right down to the bass viol wear chevrons on their sleeves.

Most of the officers dance well and there is a bet
at the bar on whether Miss So-and-so in the peasant blouse
is all her own or stuffed. The stakes run low and
the imagination high and no one has asked her yet, but
the evening has only started. And who should mind
a little camouflage, we have so much of it.

The silver dollars disappear like the moon
and we go home, no one much wiser. What happened in
the Pacific today, does anyone know? But we're
getting a grand piano from Fox who buys five or six
a year and won't miss one. Besides, we're saving
them thousands by shooting the field, and the cadets
complain about shooting in their spare time.
Who is shooting besides Fox, and what does a Fox
know of foxholes.

Who threw the little Joe and how many bucks on
the come bet?

That's our hero from Guadalcanal, he'll never be
the same. Neither will the other 'boys'. They'll
have too much or too little and you get used to
anything.

The war can't end yet. It has produced no great
music.

ARE WE ALONE

Are we alone who scan the sky for rain,
a fat and Falstaff cloud
    and a damned star,
a ready wind wrapping the desert
    and the sand still,
never counting on one hand,
never counting at all?

THE SPELLING LESSON

You know I really believed that stuff,
that if your initials spelled something,
you'd be rich? So starting out with
an L and an A and an R, I threw all
those sheep's eyes (that's what we called
the hungry look) at that young Klinger
boy. I don't know how he knew all
he knew. Surely his older brothers
couldn't have taught him all. But
I am glad he was part of my growing
up. For I truly loved him, and he me,
there for several days that spring,
and summer. And we were warm and tender
and trembled when we saw each other coming.
And would walk hand in hand around the little dark
town and anticipate. As for simple love,
there is none better.
                              Years later,
in a mess hall in Las Vegas,
catching a bite before our towing
target run, I said to my co-pilot,
"There is the back of a neck I recognize."
She called me crazy, said she didn't care
to fly with me again. We made a bet.
And when he walked out of that mess hall,
he was my young man beginning with K.
Who would have made me a LARK
to fit my flight pattern, but
he was already married to a girl
named Louise, or Lucy, or Anne with an E,
and I had made a word of my initials
and they all spelled LARD.
                              The point,
back then, was to become rich.
And that is what we were, of course,
in the middle of the Great Depression
between those two World Wars,
corn at 2¢ a bushel, clean and shelled.

FLIGHT AS A WAY OF LIFE

I used to tow targets
out of Las Vegas.
Canaries sang in their cages
in the gilded gaming rooms
not cheep, cheep, cheep but
    dear, dear
and early in the morning
when the sun struck gold into
    Boulder Lake,
there was their great golden
    egg.

TRANSFORMED

Twice on the reasonable side of dead,
I tried to recoup what the wise men said,
tried to recover the reason why
we're set on the earth to live and die.

Twice on the reasoning side of gone,
I tried to recall what was going on
when spinning began in this holy space,
how we came to be anchored in this lent place.

Twice in moments en route to dying,
I've been too close, alone and flying.
I expected bells. It was banshees crying.

But twice in moments of dreadful peace,
I knew the power of sheer release.
The answer was there within my eye.
    I forgot it all when I didn't die.

GOODBYE B-26

For a lark we were playing anteater
out in the desert, making fun
of the snout-nosed airplane equipment
meant to save our lives. O, we did laugh
and pose with those oxygen masks
pointing to the sand, and there
in the rubble behind the hangar
was the stencil for the future. . . used.
    The speed was so high that we were
    as obsolete to fight that war
    as anteaters, which weren't funny anymore.

Mickie Carmichael
44-W-4

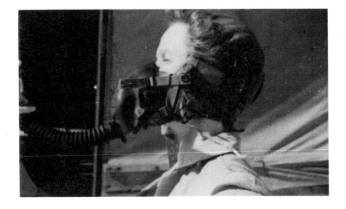

BETWEEN BATTLES IN THAT SOMETIME WAR

Twenty actual dollars went into the kitty
as the train careened along.
We were hysterical with relief
that the loss was one we could afford, sustain
without any loss of virtue or virginity.
Hail! hail! hail! oh we did blunder
and fuss and flirt, but we were mindful of what
we had to lose. . . our own hot breath.

GUSSIE SENDS QUICK LETTER

Dear Orlando, Sometimes I remember
when you tried to send me one rose
just after the geranium gas and the one
that smelled like cucumber
when we inched our way into that old house
and quick took off our gas masks
and quick put them back on
so we would know if we smelled anything funny
just what we were dying of,
                              and I guess
if you'd ordered a funeral wreath
or a bushel of cucumbers they would have
sent them but one rose they said no to
and that was the end of us. Love, Gussie.

HANGAR NINE

*Upon receiving an invitation to place my name in a
time capsule at the dedication of Hangar Nine as an
aerospace museum because I flew with the Women's
Airforce Service Pilots – known as the WASP*

". . . place your name in a time
capsule. . . aerospace shrine. . .
dedication of Hangar 9. . ."
The morning mail condenses me
into part of the blue I want to become.

I dive to the bottom
of my old trunk
to retrieve my silver wings.
I come up goggle-eyed.

I put on another hat
black cherries with a veil
and Winston Churchill is dead
in the great cathedral.
"They buried the trees
when your flyers came over. . .
let us eat our fill of strawberries
before they ploughed the berries under,
and to make the runways,
they cut and buried the trees."

The cherry-tree leaves are cherry red
and I am wearing black cherries for the dead
no, I am bareheaded
        and Wiley Post has crashed in our front hall
        black patch and all. I learn
he traded his eye for his plane
(all right, used the insurance money),
The headlines are squirming in the sun.
It is the Ides of August and Alaska has

brought him down. Not alone. Will
Rogers went down with him,
who never met a man he didn't like.

Wiley Post, born on a bloody date. . . a November
twenty-second. . . when a crashed career
drained the rest of us of dreams we'd been afraid
to dream since childhood. . . that God
was with us after all, that faith
and courage weren't misspelled words
in a computer, and suddenly
joy was splitting apart like
old chicken entrails where my grandmother
ground off the chicken head with her heel
and threw the spastic body in the dust
that August afternoon where I, crouched
in the grape vines, stiffened like death
when the headless body went by. . . it was –
Wiley Post, and I knew I was going to fly.

      "place your name in a time capsule,"
just what I've been trying to do. My time
capsule was to be a poem to wrench your lungs.
Now here it all is so simply. . . because,
because, one January deep in snow,
an Alaskan day in Manhattan,
I thought I'd learned the reason
      I learned to fly.
I made my gesture to save Paris.
I thought that Paris was where
I was trying to go.
THE GERMANS HOLD THE CITY OF LIGHT!
and copying the English girls
who pulled on helmets, parachutes
and boots and took to air, I threw
my lot in with the flyers.

47

WAR is now a dirty word
and I am marching marching.
When did WASP turn into
an obscenity? We flew
with honor for a cause:
people were being burned in furnaces,
human skin made lampshades exquisitely thin,
we cannot sit by. . .
"place your name in a time capsule"
would Will Rogers have liked Hitler?

"Lucky Lindy, flew all alone, in a little
plane all his own. . ." and I am pumping
the player piano in my gramma's cold parlor
and playing a saxophone. . . discarded by
my brother, who paid for it with nickels
and found he wasn't musical.
And I am standing leaden, astonished,
in the great Smithsonian hall, learning
for the first time that Lindbergh, flying
the Atlantic, could not see out.
There was no windshield! no windshield
at all! I wanted to run to tell somebody,
my god, what this man has done, he flew
into the unknown, blind as Wiley Post's eye,
blind as a headless chicken. But that was long ago,
and great drafted birds are flying over,
I hear their drone, and what one man has done
makes no matter. We are all flying blind.

    Place your name. Amelia Earhart
    with a touseled head was more than
    a set of rawhide suitcases.
        I had a haircut like that when
        gramma cut it under a bowl
        and all those fat curls

lay on the floor as if they had been killed.
Did she die alone? Everyone dies alone.
Amelia Earhart. . . lost at sea. . . lost at sky,
coming on with a meaning
she never intended. . . luggage, luggage.
I wish that I could recreate her skin.
Bid her walk into a room again.
God, what a dream she must have had.

Papa's hand was big and warm to hold mine
when we watched the eyes of heaven,
eyes of Mother, and God, and maybe
        Abraham Lincoln.
I once knew a German boy who said
he had drunk from the Big Dipper.

And Michael Carmichael in her cocked hat
flew all the way to hell and back while cancer ate
her heart. Impossible! The impossible happens
all the time. Walk on water. . . walk on the moon.
        Kitty Hawk, Kitty Dove, Kitty Hawk.
        Go fly a kite!
        and those bicycle brothers did.
        they made their own music.
        You can still hear it,
        if your ear is cocked
        right in the cockpit.

Place your name. Edward White. Gus Grissom. Neil Armstrong.
Amelia Earhart. Wiley Post. Lindbergh. Orville. Churchill
Lincoln. Socrates. Icarus. God.
Beelzebub. Papa. Place your name.

Freud might have said mine was a death wish
to join the conglomerate blue, that it was

heaven I meant to reach, not Paris,
that wanting to place my name
        is grandiose.
   I place his name, Freud.

       We walk in space every day of our lives
       and our name is on that piece of space where
       we bolster the air, and live it however
       we dare,
             and dream of flying.

LOGBOOK TURNED TO FEATHERS

LOGBOOK TURNED TO FEATHERS

In the dream my logbook turned to feathers
and I flew

close formation with a band of angels
flying home.

We did wingovers under bridges on the Nile
and pylon eights around the Taj Mahal.

Wingtip to wingtip we headed for the sun
with visibility

unlimited of planets yet unknown.
In a blaze

that seared my eyes to blisters
they were gone

through gates I could not follow
and I fell

through haze, through clouds, through time.
I could not tell

whether the gates were heaven or
were hell,

but I was caught in Leonardo's gaze
and Goddard's skull was tolling like a bell.

I WILL HAVE NO IDOLS BEFORE ME

On learning that Charles Lindbergh is dead

Charlie is my darling, my darling,
my darling, oh Charlie is – was
and now he has slipped into that
atmosphere that held him so chivalrously,
until we all could hold him in our arms,
call him brave, enduring and ours.
Charles is a strange name for an idol.

They read, of course they read. Didn't
the DesMoines Register and Tribune come
every day delivered by a knickered boy
being dragged around by a great canvas bag?
sometimes my brother, sometimes my cousins?
Was it my fault the only books in the house
were Horatio Alger and the Tarzan Series?
and (beside my Papa's bed) the Dream Book
and the Bible which were also dare-devil books.

And in that movie house, divided by the royal
light beam down the center aisle, came
all of those hard-riding, hard-loving
heroes, while heroines dressed as Tom Mix
swung from the chandeliers, to knock
out the villain in a double-footed whammy
and my god how we cheered! Was it any wonder

when the choices were actually made,
I decided quilt-making wasn't for me, tho they said
I made the evenest, daintiest stitches
on the block. I didn't want to wake up
in the night forty years later listening
to a train whistle. I didn't even want
to marry the engineer. I wanted to fly
the train.   Ah, Charlie!

ORDERS

After I ran away from home and came back again,
my Papa said, Go if you must but mind three things:
stay away from water, stay off of boats, and don't
go up in an aeroplane.   So first I learned to swim,
then I learned to sail,   and then I learned to fly.

THE BAGLEY IOWA POEM

1.

Bagley meant to be
a railroad town
but the railroad
hadn't heard.

Three churches
poulticed
600 people,
(five ninety-nine
after I ran away).

The sneaky holy-roller summer –
with Christian Endeavor
serving as the dating bureau –
on Main Street sat the Methodist madam.

God's sparrow
never flew in our trees
and the angling birch
filling my window
turned into a creaking skeleton
when I became
homesick at home.

2.

No was a great big
thousand letter word
and the consequences
were plenty.

Yes was love
and all that
meant, soured
and scourged
with unhappy knots
that tied the men

to their women
and the women
to their men
and the land
heaved and buckled
and produced
2¢ a bushel
    corn
and separate rooms.

3.

Bagley
well, yes,
heaved on winter streets,
sweltered in the summer,
Grandma Plummer,
deaf as a post
hole,
traded the attic
for a double-carpeted
dining room
two husbands later.
I don't think I
was through with weddings
before I began but
the illustrations
were out of focus
and the hills
were full of accidents
and proposals.

4.

I fly back to my childhood
trying to get the water-tower
shape right. Shaped like a –

I sneak up on it through the trees,
the apple trees that are young
and shapely. Shaped like –

There on its long spindly legs,
the fat tub of a water-tower
towers over the splattered town

shaped like a great bruise
with the welts running like
mainstreet and over it the water tower

shaped like a Roman candle
waiting to go off if only
someone would set a match to it.

I bring my torch. Water
tower shaped like Canaveral.
Over and over I have dreamed
of seeing Bagley from the moon.

5.

Learning that the town has no more trains
                 or buses
shouldn't matter to me who will never go there
                 again but
it has put me standing on a corner
under the bus stop sign
in my new graduation suit
and a hat with a flowing scarf
of a color I can't remember
but the dust is blowing –
gum wrappers mince down the street
making their small journey –
and I am headed away.

FLY

Birds have followed us all the way.
They take to air and glide and celebrate and we
are left to dream of flying. Every night
I startle myself with my incessant glides,
knowing this time surely I am awake.
I never am. Last night I dreamed of
superior scarlet wings, after Jane
told us the blackbirds grew red
feathers for their courting stage
and molted them for parentage. Jane,
I'd told four people before I learned
your hoax. That's one trouble, I'll believe
anything. Even that this time I can surely
                    fly.

LOVE IS

a flock of birds, soaring, twisting, turning,
floating, lifting, swooping, landing, splitting into
pieces (individual birds) that can peck peck peck
before they once again unite in the flock that, rising,
goes reeling, shifting, flying (flying, that's the word
I was looking for) right out of sight.

THE SINISTER SIDE

The day after the palm reader said my love line had disappeared,
the lump appeared on the palm of my left hand.

    (the flicker has long been in my left eye)

The doctor grabbed my left arm, made a question mark of it,
and when I winced said "Frozen shoulder."

    (the left side is the dreamer)

Being left that time, I froze into no speech. I was afraid
I might go outside with no clothes.

    (turn your left ear away from the cold night wind)

As I left, I weighed my options: two worthless traveler's checks
and a borrowed umbrella.

    (I gave up all my rights)

Left, Left, You've got it now keep it, doggone it,
don't lose it!

    (left. . . left. . .)

When the corporal said "To the winds, march!"
none of us ever came back.

PUSH

Push back the rose portieres
I am coming through.
I want my turn in the Morris Chair
with the black arm button to zing
me into orbit. Escaping always,
I am in return.

     I clutch to me
the ancient evil rights, giddy
with despair. Hopeless is a water
fall of warning. Idiocy took off
on the morning breeze, misnamed
innocence.

     We wheeled and banked
against a calico sky, blazed
a trail (we thought) of possibles.
Oh we were birds and would grow
feathers in a minute.

     We heard
the sound of the tidal wave
and thought it was applause.

PLACE COUNTS

"Place counts," but I have brought
my prairie mind to this mountain
pasture. I observe the peaks.
Old mountains, they glow blue
as far as the eye can see, surround
my ann's laced grass, support
my flock of birds, where I am
power-mad. These are my mountains,
this is my sky. And the copperhead
under the porch is mine,
my Oriental reminder that I am
full of fear and ancientness
that all the analysis in the world
can only label or identify.

Great breathing heaving meadow
that incites my prairie mind
to joy, if place cannot be sky,
       I choose you.

YOU'LL NEVER REACH THE MOON

Those white swans turning pink against the bay
are much akin to mermaids, even they,
sidesaddling their sea horse, magnified at night,
are realer than these wheeling birds in flight.
Breath-white against the bluing twilight sky,
a dozen princes turned to swans sail by. . .
        Oh I believe!
You, scientist, who categorized the clouds,
numbered the winds and photographed the sun,
I'm glad you are the one, not I,
      to so have cancelled magic and the sky.

LINES WRITTEN WHILE LANDING AT LA GUARDIA

I am
spiraling
in over North
Brother Island
squinting for
Typhoid Mary's
hut, close to the
lighthouse on
the corner toward
South Brother
where those stranded
sailors spent the night
trying to attract a rescue
and drive off rats
with their scrubby fire.

I hear
the spiraling
heat coming on
through the clanking pipes
in the Nurses' Quarters
partitioned into
living quarters
for such as us,
the veterans. Pay
the rent to Mr. Pink
and try to have a baby
to zoom down-river
to Bellevue's
obstetrics
ward.
But
it was too soon.
A one-year baby
lived with us
and laid her

head on her coconut
cake because
it was shaped
like a lamb.

I hear
the drunken
ferry captain
glancing the ship
from side to side
in the ferry slip
with every docking.
He rolled
the same old ferry
right on to Riker's
on visiting days
for the prisoners.
We were all
prisoners trying
to love
something,
trying to
attract
a rescue.

HOMING PIGEON

Scoffer, throw these feathers in the air,
watch them climb to limber wings for flight,
circle once, and then begin to soar
toward home, and you will know again delight
of naked showers in an evening rain
when you owned all the world and you were nine.

That this small skin of bird,
carried here inside a padded box
could sail up skyward, turn its head
and skim its body home, unlocks
the door to where the plan is stored.
Olympus is your home and you, a god.

THE IMAGE

I have escaped. I hover here
astride this little dollar sign,
this unidentified flying object
in disguise. (Want to see

an inside loop?) It's hard to say
just how I got away. I'll try.
Remember when we changed
from daylight saving time?

Somehow I wedged myself in the vacant
hour, and was gone before anyone knew
I was going, even me.

I have always appeared to hover,
so this position is vaguely recognized
as I angle in to those who care
to see me. (I have lost

all fear of quicksand and
the carpenter ants which haunted
my past.) Here I am only concerned
with the taller cement mountains
and updrafts of laughter.

LICKING THE DESERT

I did not know a piece of paper could bring back the desert, the dusty spice smell, the sheets of sand, blown and shifted by the wind blowing so gently, so all-the-time, that it did not seem to blow at all. The sand dust that gathered on every surface, gathered between dawn and noon, between noon and supper. Was always there. Ozymandius for me had been mostly joke and only slightly tragedy. The sand dust tried, every day on day, to cover and hide each rise and ripple that marred the smooth expanse of sand. Indeed, it would succeed. You knew it as you wiped the dust away. Your effort would cease. But the sand which came each day as surely as night filled the space between the mountains, the sand would keep coming on. In sheets of dust one after the other.

Here between the mountains that rose sharp and purple on all sides, on this flatness of sand, many men, scurrying like ants, piled board upon board for shelter for themselves and their machines. Flew their airplanes over the mountains and set them down. Shinnied the flag up its pole, and stirred the sand with their marching feet. They enlarged the countenance of the lizard and hung him over their gates. They dipped smooth rocks in white-wash and fashioned his shape on the sand. They planted green grass on a small triangular plot, and with it they planted sod, a fence, a water sprinkler and a keep-off sign for each green corner. Man was determined to lick the desert, and oh it could be done, like a great and everlasting relay race with a watering hose for the baton. But they dug sand out of the innards of their planes, and swore and sweat and cursed themselves and the army that set them down to fight the dust, the everlasting sand.

It was here I went to fly. To drive the machines that carried the men that shot the guns that hammered the target that hit the dust that gathered over everything. And at night I went back to my quarters and breathed the sand, and dreamed of sand, and knew it would gather over me before I wakened.

On such a night I scribbled words on a piece of paper. In a uniform pocket it's waited and I find it now, with the war many years over and it, too, covered with dust.

"The air is full of dust and your nose dry, and the wind with small whistles at the screen, shaking the windows. Like living in a cardboard box with the nails marching up all the walls and across the ceiling and the sand grinds under your bare feet on the wood floors, and the bulb glares in the middle of the box top with the string hanging down. The footprints show on the ceiling where men walked when the box lay another way, and now one window and a door and an iron bed and a bulb make it a house and you live in the dust and wait for the wind to blow the box over. Only the copper wire stretched from nail to nail shines in the light. Only the copper shining has life, for the part of you here is wrapped in the dust when you step in it with your feet and breathe it into your nose where the crust hardens.

Come I shall fix it into a room. Spread the brown blanket over the bed, the harsh brown blanket. Over the windows I'll hang a curtain, a rough tan curtain with splashes of red and yellow and blue. These splashes circle the holes where the bullets went through and the colored wax shows whose score was whose and highest. I shall hang a great map on the wall. The greeness and browness of it show where it leaves off at seven thousand and begins to be eight. Then we shall not hit the mountains. And the long fingers of sound filling the sky from each round tower will guide us home and we shall fear nothing. We have the mountains marked on the map. We know their names and how tall they are. Now we shall not care that the light has faded them blue and purple and then away, and the dust turned them into cardboard like our room, and the sky is gray with it and not a shining infinity black.

Why is the shooting the color and the living the gray, and when will the cardboard box blow over, so that I may run from it and not be run after. I am afraid to go outside. I shall be wrapped in dust and high shrill voices."

Reading it, the dust is dry in my nose again. But there is the copper wire stretched and gleaming! I do not know whether I can tell you of a copper wire, stretch its burnished length for you across a four-walled waste. I found it there one night, from opposite corners of the room, put up by scurrying men under orders. For such a prosaic purpose as to hang clothes upon. I saw it like seeing the home field after endless flight through storms. And I lay back on my cot and watched it gleam late in the night. It caught the night flyers' lights on the downwind leg and flashed warm and red-gold. Do you see? The dust couldn't gather and gray it out. This thread of shining metal, with the warmest of all metal lusters, stayed gleaming and warm-gold. And this thread of fire, for so it looked in the flashing night-lights, saved my quarters, my box, from gathering grayness and falling in on me.

I did not know how much this was true until the night I shuffled dog-tired home, and found the wire was gone. Clipped close to the nails at either end. Only a curling pigtail of a piece left on each wall. I found the culprit, who, discharged, going home, needed wire to fasten his luggage. How could I say, "I want my copper wire! It alone has life in this dust-filled pocket." I helped wire up the boxes and carry them down to the jeep.

FORCED LANDING

GATHER MY WINGS

There is a part of me that looks
forever for a level land
where rows of grain run
straightway to the wind.

Once you have trained
these senses, they stay trained
and though I have no need
for landing, forced or free,
this noticing is part of me,

makes me check imprecisions of an eye,
correct for choppy heartbeats,
hear a whipping tongue as dangerous.
I must go out and gather in my wings.

Once prepared for landing forced,
one lives too much alerted.
One listens for a twitch of snake,
the thud of a seedy apple.

DO YOU KNOW WHAT'S BETTER THAN
HAVING A MOUNTAIN NAMED AFTER YOU?

Keep doing those Immelman turns,
she said, but I have lost track
of Immelman. Must hunt him up or
down or find the flight text
telling how to make the track
of his turn like a cat's cradle
in air, or one of those math-
ematical excitements that has
no beginning or end or any
one plane exactly like another.
Stay amazed she said, and gave
me back my acrobatic fantasy
turning end over end
in a sky that nurtured me,
falling and feinting and climbing,
and happy as that lark whose song
may be the most beautiful sound
I have ever heard.
                  Immelman,
where are you? Where is
your moebius loop?

EVERY NOW AND THEN AT NIGHT

Every now and then at night
when a billowed cloud this side the moon
rides black and madam-like, I think of her.

Standing against the velvet draperies
in the almost pitch-dark room, she
was the only shining thing.

Bulbous woman who peddled booze
in a dry county in a checkerboard wet dry state
in a wet war country, and all

that rot-gut she sold us
should have been pure silver
for the price we paid.

And we drank ourselves to lunacy
on our one night off the base.
We knew nobody but ourselves for a thousand miles.

So we dreamed she
was our black and shining mother,
and she was.

SUGAR IN THE GAS TANK

Here in the middle of the night
propped against pillows reading
Sally Kiel's book *Those Wonderful
Women in Their Flying Machines*,
the history, the story, of our flight
with the Army Airforce planes, drowsing,
almost ready to put out the light,
I see the phrase:
         SUGAR IN THE GAS TANK.
                              I am suddenly
alerted with all the adrenaline
that ever boiled from top to bottom,
side to side, picked me up and whirled
me around and set me down as if
a tornado came suddenly to life
inside me, or a cyclone swiveled
my insides bringing me to
the fact I didn't know before, and
suddenly the dark outside my windows
is filled with enemies, the circles
of light cast by the lamps in their silk
shades become a silent adversary hunting
across my very floor for where I breathe
and feel my pulse jump, and grip my jaws
in apprehension, knowing suddenly I was
the target, and what do I do now
with my body's natural reaction. What
do I do with this adrenalin surging
through me, making me protect myself
from the enemy all around, thirty years
too late, and I didn't know him when
I saw him, didn't know that, thirty
years ago, those who were out to kill us
were gassing up our planes.

FOR A GIACOMETTI

Alberto
could put
all his
little people,
heads pin-pointed,
bodies wizened up,
in a box
and drive out of Paris
with the box
on the back
of his bicycle,
a day ahead
of the Nazis
marching in.

Whyever
did he then
enlarge
his progeny,
elongate them
into giant frames,
until the world
looked taller
everywhere,
and he couldn't
possibly escape
with his skinny
Garden of Eden
in any direction
from any enemy,
by any kind
of conveyance,
let alone
a bicycle. . .

Or did he
learn
that he had
to leave them
behind,
and that
was the only way
when he made
his last escape,
he would
ever
remain.

THE SOLDIER'S BODY ARRIVES FROM OVERSEAS

Send him, she said,
but when the train arrived,
she trembled at her door
and couldn't step outside.

Mother, they said,
you don't have to see him,
you don't have to look,
but she turned her face

toward them and shook.
I see him every night,
she whispered, he knocks,
I let him in. Who
do you suppose is in the box?

REPLY TO AN ACCUSATION

I am not Medea.
I am not even Mendel Rivers
though I drink a lot.

Your shorthand talk
has made me duck
for shelter under
poem cover.

                    I see the twister cloud
                    I know what it can do. . . run
                    straws straight through
                    a steer's hide, being worn.

          I hear a twister's roar
          under our talk. Before
          I have replied to any tense,
          you are in another cent-
          ury, hailing sensuous
          lives. I thought

                    I could fly with you but
                    my parachute is full
                    of enemies. You, free-fall-
                    ing, will out-dazzle
                    and be-shine them all.
                    Though guilt is mythical

I am not Medusa.

I am not Edith Hamilton, Viking Press,
Trader Vic, Pipi Longstocking, or the Ides
of Sears Roebuck.

I am a palm reader with no hands. . . Melpomene.

DR LEVINSON'S OFFICE DISAPPEARED SHE SAID

"Dr Levinson's office disappeared,"
she said, twisting her handbag.
Since we were standing in Doctor
Levinson's office, we knew she was
right. We did disappear for
the uncanny moment when she said
we did. The word is more than
a word. It is a pitch of blood
stream that blinks us in and out
of sight. It is a note on a hot
fiddle.

     Of course we disappeared!
Last seen flying over a high E chord
pitched beyond ear-take, sun-spot,
pitched beyond hazardous belief,
curved on melody that rises, rises
out of the Merlin-boxes, horns,
the theory of flight has taken over
sweating hands and we are rising for
there is vacuum to be filled and we
are the music, the magic, the music,
straight out of sight!
     We have disappeared.

     No no no, it was not that way at all.
It was the Emerald Shillelah Marching
and Chowder Flying Club that was to blame.
Being a charter member, Dr L was booked for
the next trip and so wasn't there when
this girl came to see him and that's only
the way she put it, phrased it, you know how –
Dr Levinson disappeared, she said, but that
was all she meant – that he wasn't there when
she wanted him.

What kind of leprechaun is Levinson?
First grade, topnotch, quality.
He can disappear at will, and only recently
has he had any trouble coming back.
That is because the protons, after
a certain age, tend to run toward
the end of the tipped-up week.

      Fools. We disappear as pain
does. You can't remember pain however
hard you try. There is the doppler effect
like eerie train whistles. . . and the further
off, the further off, and after a while
when you say "Pain" it is only a red neon
sign blinking on and off. The pain
has disappeared. Our insides wipe
it out. And we disappear. In pieces.

Dr Levinson, Dr L, she said, just before
      she disappeared.

NO RIGHT

What can I do to feel close to you?
Put on something belonging to you –
your long blue cape embroidered
       with blood.

I am flying into the sunset
too many times. I am speeding
west and on this day I have seen
       seven sunsets.

The sun is always going down,
we are rounding the corner speeding,
there is an aura of color –
       splintering glass.

Suicide is for the upper class.
Down here there are only accidents,
a hunting episode, the speeding car,
       the startled ditch.

But where are the children of the oven
breathers? Child of the slashed wrists
where are you – of the heavy accelerator
foot – child of the barbed wire face –
       here in this ditch mama here.

AN OLD FILM AT THE REUNION OF THE FIFINELLAS

I watch the girl,
hair flying,
leap onto the wing
of an AT-6.
I know who she is,
I have made that leap.
I watch those planes
in formation,
precede their moment
of peeling off
with a delicious
NOW
and pull away,
my body arcing,
that small smile
coming up from
my toes
and settling
on my mouth.
O clear arc
in the air,
when did I begin
forgetting
I can fly?

A BURIAL PLOT

The Secretary of Defense says:
(35 years late) "Congratulations,
Women of the Airforce. . ." So what
do we get after all those years of
struggle? Recognition and a Burial Plot.

To be shut off from Roundelay Farm
is to know a little of being
turned out of the Garden.
It has been my Eden, complete
with Satan, the snake who
crushed the ferns with his body
and brought down night with
his tongue.

I love that piece of land,
every wildflower plant I have
transplanted, the kitchen floor
I laid, graced with wildflowers
painted by friends who have
come and gone. I know
the bloodroot is beginning to bloom,
the hepatica grins from under
a pile of leaves, the anemone
and the meadow rue are waiting for
the word "Go" and in a week or
two, spring beauties will
turn the ground to pink
before your very eyes.

I have been cut off from the land
I learned to love, cut off
from the mountains that lift up

and bringeth my help. Cut off
from the family burial plot.
I have been cast off to bobble
on the rapids, clutching my poems.

I have just decided not
to be buried anywhere.

THE HEARING 11/2/77

For Lindy Boggs & Margaret Heckler
Women of Congress

Today I watch you move
in that body which makes
laws, see you curb your anger,
your dismay, always with grace,
knowing you stake your future
halfway between Woman and
whatever brought you to this place,
aware of hurdles only women
have to leap. (Look if you
like, said Auden, but you have
to leap.) And to establish
what you take for Right.

Rights! Ah sisters who have reached
beyond the coffee cups and slid
past patting hands. You have
taken up our cause (which I
had doubts about. . . Just let
it go. . . we served. . . as everybody
served. Live ammunition, yes,
for sure, of course) but you
engage live ammunition now
from men who run the world.

You will be shot down
and rise again and smile, until
we reach again the Eden speech
before the Babel Tower
sprung us into languages
where men spoke one,
and women spoke another
even in same tongues.

(And women had to know men's
languages to teach their sons.)

Ordered not to speak,
now sisters together,
our tongues untied,
    we fly.

WING-TIP TO WING-TIP

And now I feel again the flight
wing-tip to wing-tip, the delicious
shift, the singing swinging power
of peeling off in formation and
zooming home, only to join again
in careful delicate ways. My god
exactly *exactly* like the poem-making
with the lines, wing-tip to wing-tip
and the careful feeling to put them
all in place, to hold them there,
the same delicious power when
the line, the word, is balanced
against the next, the one ahead
and the one behind, and the one
beside, and it is very akin
to love.

I *will* remember that the crying
and the laughing is only formation
flying, balance myself against my own
inexorable needs and take off over and
over again for as many days as I can
manage. Curiosity is in my marrow,
risk, my aim, and if there is love,
and I think there is, I'll find it
and fly it home.

I walk again through those maneuvers,
buckle my parachute, and climb in my plane.
It is the only way to begin.

CLEARED FOR APPROACH, CLEARED FOR LANDING

1.

If you draw the vectors down the middle sky
translating them as you go to wind velocity,
accelerated heartbeat, awakened belief
in a trail of blood, blood on the salt-lick,
blood on the high grass, blood on the oat-trough,
you come to the heaving ram in the field,
a mound of sodden wool, his face torn and hanging,
and the vectors cross in your gut while your eye
catches the skulking sight of the dog turned wolf
slinking away through the trees. The cold sun sinks.
Bobbing lights bring on the veterinarian
to stitch the stricken sheep
before its breath goes out.
Dark overtakes him.

> Was it a slaughtered lamb?
> Were we to make some sacrifice?
> What have we done to this
> mounded meadow, broken some
> wilderness code, pretending
> we are civilized?

514 How do you read?

2.

Through the window above the kitchen sink,
past the log pile stanched between two trees,
past bare branches of dogwood, hickory,
splashing against winter skeletons
is the blare of your red coat and I freeze
with the dishcloth in my hands, freeze
with terror of the familiar.
What do I know that I cannot know?

Once in a movie of clairvoyance,
spilled black ink turned red,
and the father, running,
found only a red coat floating,
all that was left of his own
Red Riding Hood. Your red coat
floats through the trees. I know
you are digging a grave.
I have no clue to what terror floats toward us.

> We move in time as we can.
> The signals always come on,
> they drift into focus and out
> and sometimes in orange-red light
> we see them clearly crossing
> on a blood-soaked woolen coat
> like our own sheep in his field.
>
> I am wearing my own red coat.
> There is blood on the salt-lick,
> blood on the trough. A low growl
> forms in my throat.

514 How do you read?

3.

Church time, Sunday morning.
The electricity has gone off,
the sky has come down.
Fog envelopes the house,
moves in great clouds across
the meadow. In our eyes the winter trees
come and go, in our ears, the roar
of engines magnifies, too close too close.
Swooping, it comes and goes
and we know. . . we know.

We know nothing.
The house has turned cold.
We freeze in knowledge
and move on again.
The knowing moves in great clouds across
the meadow, comes and goes.
We do not want to know what we know.

4.

My depth perception melted years ago
as I was hanging clothes, when my fingers
reached beyond the clothesline.
Reach exceeding grasp is no good
in a capsule plane. Accuracy is everywhere
or there is no anywhere.

At eleven 09 on Sunday morning
the plane droned low over our house.
Twenty seconds later it flew into Weather Mountain.

I am not responsible. I have accurately
figured that I could not have reached
the telephone, called the field, alerted
the crew. The moment of crash is exact.
The speed of aircraft is recorded. Twenty
seconds is not enough time to reach up
my hand in the air and stop that flight.
Now you know who I think I am. And
guilty of everything.

Madness lies
in a route into Weather Mountain.
The Great Observer watching it all,
becoming the Great Not-Quite?
My life passed before me in the middle
of the fog on Sunday morning
and made a bee-line for the peaks.
Flew into a mountain. With all
aboard singing and dancing
and the altimeter working, after all,
and the flight path accurate
and the hearing optimal. So what
of the rain and the wind and the fog?
Under that throttle is power, and with
that power we flew into Weather Mountain.

A head is hanging
in a tree. Firemen hunt
for bodies. I wonder about
the fingerprints when
the fingers are forsaken.

I am guilty, Jesse Glass, of not replying.
Hallucinations haunt my dreams
and your robed monk disappears over and over
through the wrinkle at the end of night.

514 How do you read?

11:09:55
TWA 514 from Dulles Approach. Tell me your altitude.

11:10:01
Trans-World 514 Dulles. How do you hear?

11:10:12
TWA   TWA Five One Four, Dulles Approach. Do you read.

11:10:24
TWA 514 Dulles. One Two Three Three Two One.
How do you hear me?

11:10:30
TWA Dulles. Do you read?

11:10:44
TWA 514 Dulles. One Two Three — Three Two One.
How do you hear me?

11:11:08
TWA 514 514 Dulles Do you read? How do you read?

> Only the fog reads.
> The rain puts out small fires.
> There are several minutes
> up against the mountain
> when only the flames and the fog and the rain
> move. Everything else is still.

6.

LET ME ASK YOU ONCE AGAIN, CAN
YOU CLARIFY

*(Can you resurrect? Speak in tongues?
Join the proper arms and legs to the proper torso?)*

AS NEAR AS YOU REMEMBER, EXACTLY
WHAT DID YOU SAY AND DO?

*(Crawled around the floor hunting the plane,
Crawled around my head hunting my last words,
where was the plane, I called and called and
no one answered. I called where are you, he
was right there in my picture, right there
on my slate, I could see him wave, he was right
there, see, there, but he wouldn't call back
to me, he wouldn't even answer, and I told him
allyallyocks in free, but he wouldn't come
and I yelled and hunted him and he wouldn't
come, and for spite he splattered himself
on the mountain. I called him to come home
but he wouldn't come.)*
I cleared him for approach.

IS IT TRUE THAT YOU CLEARED THE AIR-
PLANE FOR FINAL LANDING?

Oh no. I cleared him for approach. *(I cleared
him to come home free, allyallyocks, I said.)*
I cleared him for approach, not for landing.

WOULD YOU CLEAR UP THE MATTER OF
THE DIFFERENCE BETWEEN APPROACH
AND LANDING?

Approach is coming into the flight pattern,
the necessary flying configuration at a specific
level. . .

ALTITUDE?

Altitude. *(and you fly that altitude until I say*
you can't. I tell you what to do, and I told him
to come home. Dammit. Why was he coming anyway?
We weren't expecting him. Why didn't he fly to
Timbuktoo or Baltimore? No one belonged
on that runway. Nobody ever lands there,
it could have grown over with grass and floated ducks
for all we knew. It wasn't fit to fly that day,
even the ducks were walking, as they say, and oh god,
I can't help everything, doesn't anyone realize that?
that the body is alive, oh god, alive alive ally, alack,
alive's in free, I'm free, I'm free. Why didn't he
come when I called him?)

CAN YOU HELP CLARIFY APPROACH AND
LANDING?

There's the approach and then there's the landing
approach. *(anybody knows that — it's clear enough —*
anybody knows)

AND IF YOU SAY CLEARED FOR APPROACH DOES
THAT MEAN APPROACH TO THE FIELD OR
APPROACH TO THE GROUND?

It means whatever there is to do next. *(It means*
exactly what it says. You're trying to confuse me.
I'm free you know. I came in free, I freely came
to testify.) I'll tell you anything you want to know,
What do you want to know?

DID YOU KNOW THERE WAS A MOUNTAIN THERE?

No.

7.

From here you can see the course
the plane took. Huge splintered
trunks stand upright, forming
the shape of the plane.

An icy wind rattles paper caught
high in a standing tree. A small
woodpecker is sending a coded message.

Under my foot is a piece of
pleated fusilage, wedged so tight
under rock, only machines can
dislodge it. Machines have put
it there. Miscalculation has
put it there. Poor communication
has put it there with the horn
blowing and the pilot shouting
GET THE POWER ON. We know because
it is all there on a tape preserved
in a small orange box which records
every sound in the cockpit, in case
we need to know.

The final sound is of the crash.
It is preserved on the tape
in the small orange box.

8.

        I have flown
that sloping flight over and over
in my sleep, angling
over the Alleghenies, over the Shenandoah
headed for the building that flies
which Saarinen made for the airport.

Tonight in a wandering sleep I knew
I was not responsible, I *was* the crash.
It was my own inevitable end, to be
splattered on Weather Mountain,
and here I am kissing the ground
and picking up pieces.

9

It is said that in the FINAL CRASH
by whatever bomb is currently in operation,
Our Government will retrench
at Weather Mountain: the biggest open
secret in the East. There is a marker there
that arrows from the West – a long strip
of match-stick splintered trees – a charred
pointer. Beside that final holocaust
this crash will be but "a drop in the bucket,"
a small flint. We know and we do not
want to know what we know. Everyone
has second sight. We all wear bloody
coats, watching the dog turn wolf.
514 or any other number, do you read?
How do you read?

10.

And then it was I heard the horn
blowing through fog, and I did not cry
out, but gave all power and rose up
and cleared the mountain and the weather

and knew all that was left to me.

EVERYTHING I EVER FLEW IS OBSOLETE

All I ever flew is what brought
me here. Pavarotti did the film
and we picnicked on the Boston
Pops' green, warned not to look up
at the helicopter shooting film
like the drama of watching Father
Roseliep fall in love with Katherine
Anne Porter and her pet emerald.
I fell in love with every Clark Gable
who came along unless I was already
in love with a Leslie Howard.

We didn't mean to bring the movie down.
We loved it anyway. One woman's
success is another female's future
failure. The propellor in the living
room is no more improper than
the coffin next the fire.

CHATTANOOGA CHOO CHOO IN KALAMAZOO

The O's have it!   O how the O's
echoed in the Mood in Kalamazoo, in Chattanooga.
O how the horns moaned and the reeds melodyzed,
and the Big Band was a band with no strings ex-
cept the bass that thrummed and thrummed and
Glen Miller headed for Paris from England
and was never seen again.   OOO o ooo o

Captain Glenn Miller in '42
put together the Air Force Band,
boosted morale all over Britain. A General
balked at the St. Louis Blues March. "Sousa
was good enough for us in 1918." Glenn grinned,
"Do you still fly the planes of 1918?" Off
he flew in a fog in a single engine plane with
no de-icing equipment. His pilot said
they would fly low. Glenn said leave three
musicians, make the plane lighter. On TV
those three are alive and laughing. OOO ooo

Fifty years later few things throw
the lever for tears. Nostalgia twirls
letters, medals, photos, but swing
into the rhythm of the dancing tunes,
give me back my saxophone, give me
back my restless feet and I am dancing
through a curtain of water raining
as if my heart could break. . . OOO O ooo o

A PLAY IN FIVE FICTIVE VOICES

FINAL FLIGHT CHECK

Cast: Samantha (All are women of the WASP)
                Tyler
                Dolly
                Bridey
                Ruth

Scene: Avenger Field Flight Line, Sweetwater, Texas
                Fliers in Zoot Suits (Olive green coveralls)
                Fliers lined up on bench waiting their turns

Sound: Chorus of Women's voices singing:
                Zoot Suits and Parachutes

> Zoot suits and parachutes
> and wings of silver too
> he'll ferry planes
> like his Mama used to do.

The characters in this play are fiction, based on action and reaction that might have happened, placed in a real setting, during and after WWII.

SAMANTHA: Women have stood in this spot before, but not me, and not many. This is a new slice of excitement and anxiety. I will not think Washout. I will not think about what happens when this afternoon is over. It will be Total time – total Triumph or Despair. I will think only Now, Now. Or back then –

I will think about the one and only time I ever flew by myself over Manhattan. It was the first week I was in New York. From Iowa to New York. I took the subway out to a little field on Long Island called Idlewild – Yes, that is what it was called before it became Kennedy Airport. They looked at my license, checkchecked my physical, gave me a map and said: (very fast) You can't fly here and not over there, and don't cross there – pay your money at the cashier – Go check out a Taylorcraft at the Second Hangar. And I did.
All by myself over Manhattan! I was so busy trying to keep out of the air space I wasn't supposed to be in that I hardly had time to enjoy it. I figured if I did trespass, some Big Gun would shoot me down, or a big American Eagle would swoop down and snatch me up.

I really just wanted to see Manhattan from the sky, how the rivers ran, and the Statue of Liberty with her light – that was one place I was supposed to avoid. Oh but it was a glorious feeling, sitting up there in my little plane flying over the biggest city in the world and I was bursting with joy. I'll remember that flight my whole life, no matter what happens today.   Coming!

(Blackout)

TYLER: Yes, you probably heard right. I keep a knife under my pillow. What else is new? I don't trust anybody. They issue these big orders: NO FRATERNIZING WITH INSTRUCTORS. Who would want to is what I'd like to know. If they were worth a bag of beans they'd be overseas flying where it really counts. Such a poor excuse for males I've never seen. OFF-LIMITS TO MALES – that's the sign out front of the barracks. But I'm not taking any chances. If anybody – I mean ANYBODY– comes around here I'm going to protect myself. And it wouldn't be the first time either.

I've had to protect myself ever since the old man moved back in with us. Ma let him come back which was a whopping mistake. But he'd busted his leg riding in the rodeos and it never healed right, he said. The heel part was him. Seemed he limped when he needed to. And he was all right as long as he was sober. I really think that was the story – not the leg bit – the way he told it. I think they probably fired him because he was drunk all the time and when he got drunk he got crazy. I remember some times – but I better not tell all I know. Sometimes I didn't even think he could be my Pa. He'd taken off when I was too young to remember – and we'd lived alone all those years with Ma working at the restaurant and me too doing errands I was big enough for. She seemed to like it when he came back so I tried not to complain.

I began to spend more and more time with the pilots who came into the restaurant – listening to them talk flying. I couldn't wait till I was old enough to get my license. I tried to finagle this one guy into teaching me early on. Turned out that's not what he wanted to teach me. Maybe you get the idea how I don't trust anybody.

112

Actually there was this one fella – he was a piano player. He was with the orchestra they brought in from Big Spring for a graduation dance. I did like him. I liked him a lot. He was gentle and sort of funny lookin', he wasn't like any guy I ever knew before. One of his eyes was blue and the other was almost brown, so he had a kind of doggy look that made you do a double-take. When he went back to the West Coast, he sent me a wire: J'taime. I didn't even know what that meant. Deaver told me it said "I love you" in French. I wired back: "Go back you fool, you'll never make it." You know, for luck! That's what we used to yell at the gals lined up ready to take off. Like "break a leg" to an actor. You never meant break a leg. Well, I guess he didn't get it, because I never heard from him again.

I know I can pass this check ride if the Major gives me half a chance – if he doesn't hold it against me that I'm awkward, knobby kneed and almost too tall to get in. Under the height reg, I mean. I know I'm funny looking, but it doesn't affect my flying. I'm a good pilot.

I don't know whether you know it or not, but there are a lot of guys who don't want us here. Just because we are women. I can't understand that. We can fly as well as they can, they just have this thing about women doing work that has been men's dominion. I can ride a horse as well as any man I know. I can shoot skeet as well as any man, and I'd have a gun under my pillow if it weren't illegal. They didn't say anything about knives.

And last week I heard, get this, they have this new big plane that has some bugs in it, and the fellas refused to fly it, so the Commandant at this field had one of the biggies flown in – and out stepped these two young women – smart as you please – filed a flight plan and got back in their B-29 and took off. No more trouble with the guys! Ha!

It's sort of like our going from PTs to Advanced. We just skipped the BT-13 – Basic – until we came back for instruments. Boy what a let-down to fly that old klunker after the AT-6. But they figured if we could go from PTs to ATs the men could. Guinea pigs, that's us. That's all right with me. I don't care. I like to fly and I'll probably go on flying the rest of my life. Maybe get my own field. Maybe get my old man to stake me. He ought to be good for something.

(Blackout)

DOLLY: Dear God (Eyes closed, her hand clutching the small cross hung around her neck) Dear God, let it happen. Let me make it. I've got to fly for him. Dear Gary, I've got to fly in your stead. Bless me, wherever you are, ride with me. Make me do it perfectly. Dear God take care of him in your heaven. And please God let me make this final check ride.

(To audience) I'll tell you how it was. We were both golden kids. We grew up on the same street in Santa Monica. Our fathers both worked for Metro Goldwyn Mayer. Our life was like a movie, an Andy Hardy movie. Everything we did turned out right – until – well, the crazy part was that we looked enough alike to be brother and sister, blue-eyed tow-heads, curly haired, snub-nosed. I have pictures of us playing in the garden hose, naked as jaybirds, swimming at Laguna. We were as familiar with each other's body as any two people could be. When we were married, there wasn't any mystery, we just went on enjoying each other. We were both 18. Now that I think of it, those years of body awareness were probably a big help when I started drawing for Disney. Of course, I'd had lessons since I was seven or eight. It was bodies I drew first, even if there weren't any angels in the drawing I was making, I'd add a few putti, that's what they called it in art school. I'd doodle cupids on all of my books, even now I think of the wings I put on them. I never connected it to my flying until now. I did think of their being my guardian angels, and if I ever needed a guardian angel, it's now.

Drawing got me the job with Disney. They hired so many artists, I was just one of a corp, but it felt special, drawing for the man responsible for all that laughter. It fit right in with our golden childhood.

115

Little did I know that he would draw us our own special symbol – our Fifinella! Oh yes, he drew it just for us. It's the big sign over the gate to Avenger Field, didn't you see it? The helmeted woman with her wings and boots. It's our flight patch on our flying jackets. It was his gift to the War effort. I don't say this to just anybody but somehow that flying woman is me! She even looks like me, sort of. No, she's our guardian angel and I need her now. I have to pass this flight test. I have to fly in Gary's place. You see, he crashed in an Army plane six months ago. We'd only been married a year and two months and four days. It was a terrible storm, he hadn't even been in battle at all. He was still in training. And now I have to take his place. He would have wanted me to.

(Golden light dims slowly)

BRIDEY: (Singing) Round heels, round heels,
we're Major Gerber's sluts!
Round heels, round heels,
we're happy in our ruts,
tra-la-tra-la-tra-la-tra-la. . .

So! Did you hear our new theme song? The Major
hit a flat chord when he made the mistake of address-
ing us as Round Heels. This was in his lecture last
week: (solemnly, deep voiced) I have learned from
unquestionable sources of WASPs consorting with
Instructors, and with visiting Cadets from nearby
bases. This is to stop immediately. I will have no
Round Heels in my command! Well! Some of us
didn't know what round heels meant – and had to be
told – an easy pushover backward in position. Some
of us thought it was pretty funny, that he would use
that term. And others were steaming! I never saw
Tyler so mad! Anyway we decided to go along with
his assessment of us, so we used it as our marching
song. Round heels, round heels, to breakfast, lunch,
dinner, flight line until the order came down from on
high: Cease and desist! or demerits would arrive
from every singing note.

So I have to sing it quietly: (demonstrates) R H, R
H, we're Major G's sluts, R H, R H, we're happy on
our butts – tra-la tra-la. . .

I don't know what they expected of a baseful of
healthy young bodies and souls, active in every way.
Just because we were female? They certainly made
appropriate romantic plans for the young gentlemen
up the road at Lubbock and Big Spring – lectures on
how to avoid disease, pregnancy, etc., etc. Did they
think this little enclave of female types was going to
be happy sitting on our hands? I don't mean me. I'm
married. I'm going to stay as faithful to Gordy as I

can. But most of these young things are mighty glad to see a truck-load of cadets landing for a dance, even if all the music is juke-box, tho I think if I hear another nasal "Paper dolly to call my own" I'm going to be tearing more than paper. But even us old marrieds like a little male companionship now and then, and I for one like to dance up a storm every chance I get.

And speaking of storms, one nearly knocked me out not long after I got here. It was our wedding anniversary. Gordy was off on his Destroyer. We had a clue arrangement so I'd know where he was, but the enemy wouldn't. But I hadn't heard from him yet. I was feeling very lonely for him. Tyler and I watched the great sunset and the stars come on like a diamonded tent – the stars are bigger than any back East – But we were trying to keep words like wash-out, crash, submarines, kamikaze – out of our thoughts. Kamikaze was a new word. The concept of being taught to take off and never being taught to land hadn't occurred to us before the war. Anybody with a good right arm could take off in a plane. Nothing to it. And almost any ship was a fair target. Kamikaze talk about destroyers! A Destroyer ship didn't have a chance in hell against a humanized, mechanized, suicidal kamikase! Never taught to land! A human bomb!

But that night, I didn't even know Sweetwater had a florist. Until the flowers arrived. My favorite gardenias and cornflowers. The color of sky and the color of clouds, and I loved the gardenia perfume. So that's what arrived for our anniversary. Trouble was the florist box didn't come until after dark. There was a tap on the door and Ethel, she was on duty that night, handed me this florist box. I opened it up – all its rainbow tissue paper, and there they were! I danced around the cement floor, giving each of my baymates a whiff, but it was after lights-out and the barracks were hot as a furnace. I knew those flowers would just wither up in that heat. The outside was a little cooler, so I set the box outside the bay door, with a rock on top so it wouldn't blow away. But I hadn't counted on a Texas Wind Storm! In the night it began and as soon as I heard it, I ran for the door, but I was too late. The box was gone! At the crack of daylight, I went hunting – nothing. I never saw those flowers again. All I ever found was a scrap of rainbow tissue paper caught on the corner of a barbed wire fence way off at the far end of the field. I was hot and covered with dust and sweat and it was as if I would never be clean again. As if all of my femininity nad been wiped away with that hateful sand-filled wind. Disappointment swept over me. I choked on it.

(Lights are going down in a circle around the rainbow tissue paper in her hand) That's the night I named the Texas storm the Kamikase.

(Dark)

RUTH: Mail is a big deal here. But I wish I hadn't picked up mine this morning. This letter came from my cousin in New York State. She's there at a retreat for refugees. She got a boat out of Lisbon after waiting – I don't know how long – for all the right papers ... but now she's getting word from Europe, and the stories she tells... I've heard some awful stuff before – about people being herded into camps and families separated, their belongings confiscated. Some of it is true, I'm sure. Look what we've done, put the Japs in camps in Montana or Idaho somewhere away from the coast so they can't make it easy for Jap planes to come even closer than Pearl Harbor. Whoever thought they could get that close! Oh sure, old Billy Mitchell said one day the Japs would come. He even said: Some Sunday morning the Japanese would fly over Pearl Harbor and bomb it to smithereens, but nobody listened. He said that way back in '21 or '22, that's what I heard. They even cashiered him out of the Army, did you know that?

Well, it makes you wonder whether what's being said right now is true. Dora, that's my Polish cousin, says they're not just putting people in camps, they're wiping them out – KILLING – in things like gas houses. That they are told to take off their clothes, to get rid of lice or whatever, and they are pushed into shower rooms that aren't shower rooms at all. They are GAS chambers. And she says she knows this for certain – that one of her neighbor's sons – a boy about 15 – had escaped from one of these places and he swears it is true. He escaped by flattening himself under a barbed wire fence. There was another boy with him, they got separated in the woods and he doesn't know whether the other boy got out or not. He said they put dogs on the trail, but it rained a lot and the trail was lost, thank God.

Somebody in a little town nearby put him in a potato cellar long enough for him to escape. My God what kind of things are going on over there – kids having to run for their lives.

I've heard all kinds of stories, about piles of gold eyeglasses, gold teeth, anything of value from corpses, but somehow I thought they were from a bombing or something where people were killed accidentally, which isn't any better, they are just as dead, but what I mean is, it wasn't a matter of killing for killing's sake. Now, women, children, little babies, everybody! Wiping out a whole race, that's what she says they're up to.

War used to be an honorable affair, didn't it? All those grand martial pieces and poetry about fighting for one's country and honor? This isn't like that at all. This is making garbage out of human beings. What happens to their souls? Where is God in all of this? Are we created in His image or aren't we? It just makes me want to get a big plane and go bomb the daylights out of that Hitler Gang. That's what it is, a Gang of Criminals. We can't let a Madman win this war! We've got to help out somehow!

(Blackout)

SAMANTHA: So I won my wings. Those silver beauties were pinned onto my Santiago Blue Uniform. I stood at attention and my hat stayed on. That afternoon I was matron of honor at the wedding of Star and Buzz. The night before, Star's mother who had arrived from Illinois, took me aside and said "I would like you to do me a favor. Would you tell Star what she needs to know about – you know – married love?" I was dumbfounded. Star could have told me a few things.

So there were 1830 of us – 1074 who won wings. That means 756 washed out. That's more people than lived in the town where I grew up. I've heard some rumors that I don't want to believe – that there was a quota system for some classes before us – when the instructors were asked to be sure to cut the graduates by some degree. I don't want to believe that. And 37 of our women died in the service of their country, in the Army Airforce. It's nothing to brag about, but that was a better record than the men had.

After a stint at an Advanced training base in Stockton, testing planes, once delivering planes back to a factory in Texas for repairing wind-torn wings, several of us landed in Las Vegas – that neon cat of a town. There were some mapping missions out over the Indian Mountain Range. I like that – thinking of mapping land that hadn't been mapped before. But our real job there was towing targets for gunnery practice. We would take off – release from the bomb bay the long funnel of canvas to trail our plane. Along side of us would fly B-17s loaded with gunners. These young men had already been shooting at P-39s with cameras. If they had started with real bullets, they would have shot through half of our planes –

the responses were devilishly swift. Once they had the film developed, they see where they had sliced a wing or prop – and go back up and try again.

We were part of the next step. The B-17s would maneuver around us, but this time they had real ammunition. They had machine gun belts dipped in different colored wax. Red was the nose gunner, green the tail gunner, yellow and blue the wing gunners – and when we dropped the sleeve, the target, after a shooting run, they could tell by the color of the wax around each hole, which gunner had managed to hit it. Very colorful, those targets. We used them for curtains, bedspreads, anywhere we needed cloth.

Las Vegas. Of course we gambled. We had time off. But our biggest gamble was flying those targets for live ammo. Somebody always asks if we were ever hit. That was always a possibility, even though the planes we flew had an extra foot on each wing, trainer-bombers, TB-26s, and we flew without the extra gas load.

One of our WASPs was flying co-pilot on a plane that crashed on a training flight. Both pilots were killed. The first pilot's body was sent home for burial with honors. The co-pilot – well, that was another story. The Army said it was not responsible, since we were being paid by Civil Service. Civil Service said it was not responsible since we were flying under Army orders. So we took up a collection to send her body home. I didn't want to know we could be treated that way, just because we were women.

If we had been men, we would have been officers from the start. We were expected to act like officers, follow Army regulations to the letter. We were punished like officers if we stepped out of line. Dressed down, if we didn't salute. Told not to associate with enlisted personnel! But we had no benefits, no insurance, no medical rights, no education guarantees. All because the Army statutes were written in male pronouns.

We flew 60 million miles for the Army Airforce, doing what we called sometimes aerial dishwashery. When they decided to disband us, there were more men coming home from overseas than they expected, they simply announced: Your job is over. Goodbye. The war wasn't over yet. It was as if they pushed us out the bombay without a parachute.

Thirty years later, we were still trying to earn our legitimate place in history. We were still outsiders. The Veteran's Committee was awarding Veteran's rights to Polish men who fought in Europe on the Allied side. We were still denied the name of Veteran because we were female.

During the hearings, the head of the Veteran's Committee said to one of our witnesses, "I have no intention of letting this bill reach the floor of the House. I'm only listening to you because I owe Senator Goldwater a favor." We were stunned. He banged his gavel for recess. In the hall we said: "But sir, all we wanted to do was fly." I have never seen a face so contorted with rage: "That was the trouble! You wanted to FLY."

When the bill was signed on Thanksgiving Eve of 1977 in the White House, no WASPs were present. The only newspaper to carry the story the next day was the Mexico City Times.

(Final Blackout)

HELLO SPRING

Just now I have my own private robin
who is carousing around my back yard
hunting a boondoggled worm. I have named
him Harbinger, and I have come

to the kitchen to make a radish sandwich
to celebrate the arrival of the season,
sliced radish on rye, the red-rimmed
wheels on the slice of bread begin to spin

to energize the youth of the year.
While I am composing my spring song,
my head spins remembering you, who knew
all there was to know about flying,

and so while the rest of us pondered wind
velocity, and sweat through check-out rides,
you flew the whole course upside down
and had a new view of the world.

Mary Cooper Cox
44-W-3

You represent my youth to me, and so,
in this spring of the year, I could kiss
the woman who answered my 555-1212 and gave me
your telephone number and in a moment,

Mary Cooper Cox, I will hear your voice,
and my youth will be returned to me
for just the length of time it takes
Harbinger to eat his worm. *Hello!*

photo by Jackie Creative Photography

44-W-3

TOP ROW: (uniformed)

Stege, Juliette Jenner
Harvey, Maxine Manogue
Hale, Isabelle McCrae
Bent, June Braun
Lent, Kristin Swan
Nemhauser, Vivian Gilchrist

THIRD ROW:

Fleisher, Ruth Shafer (44-4)
Christian, Margaret DeBolt
Cox, Mary Cooper
Darr, Ann Russell
Anderson, Meriem Lucille Roby (44-4)

SECOND ROW:

Sieber, Delrose
Muise, Doris Duren
Young, Lois Bristol

BOTTOM ROW:

Quinlan, Mary Abbie
Welch, Norine Patterson
Paschich, Beryl Owens

Ready
Room

Ground
School

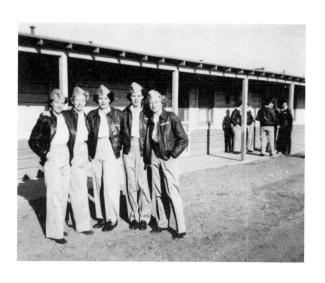

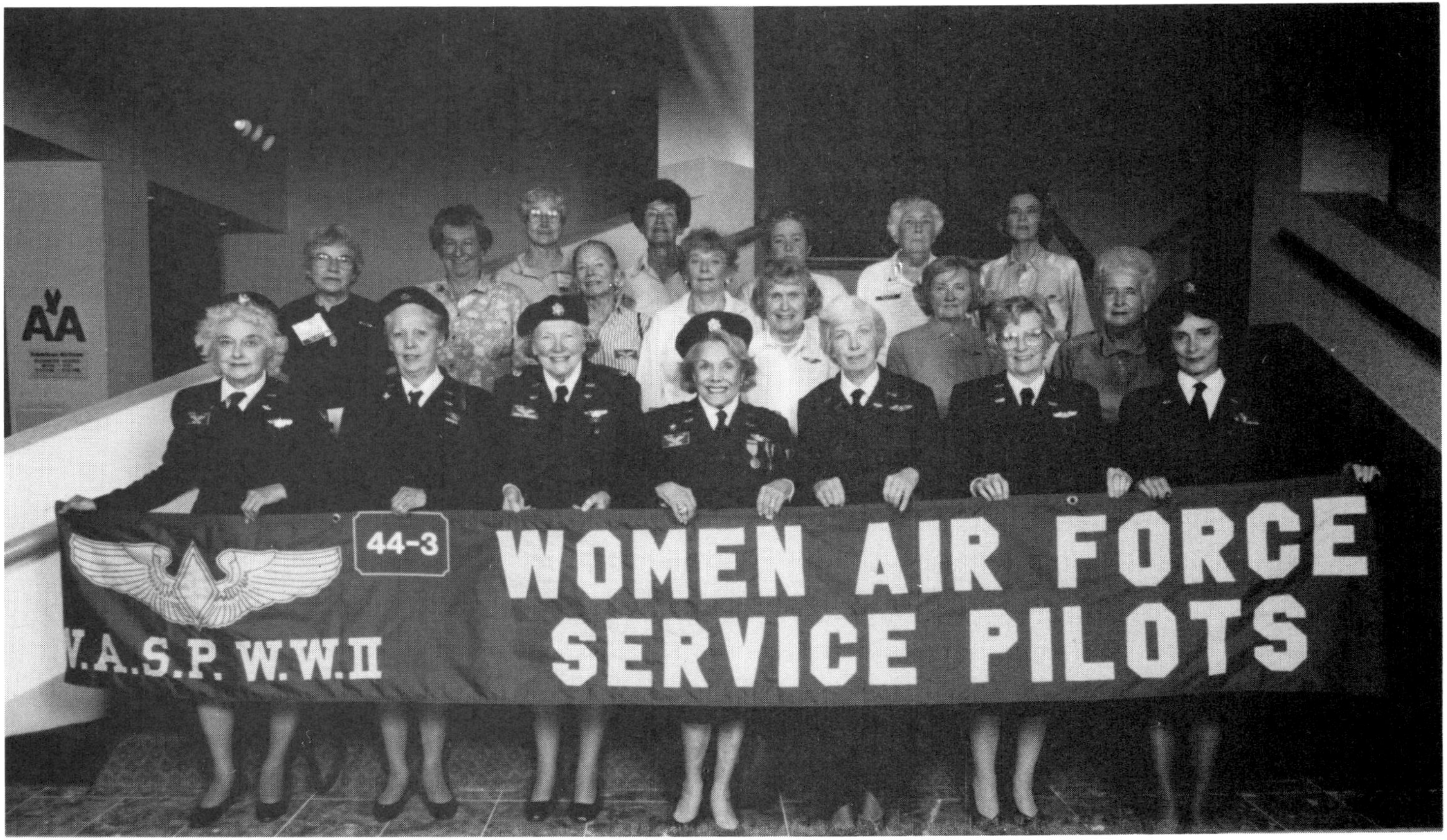
44-3
WOMEN AIR FORCE
SERVICE PILOTS
W.A.S.P. W.W.II
AA